Mexico

A Guide to the Must-See Cities in Mexico!

By Sam Spector

Table of Contents

Introduction

Hi, my name is Sam and I first of all want to thank and congratulate you for purchasing my book, 'Mexico: A Guide to the Must-See Cities in Mexico!'

Mexico is an amazing country filled with fascinating historical locations and a deep, vibrant culture. Each of the cities in Mexico offers something different to its visitors: from the sun-drenched sands of coastal cities such as Tulum, to the hectic, buzzing metropolis of Mexico City. All are unique in their own way, and have different sights and attractions to explore and enjoy.

The Mexican people are quite often reserved but overwhelmingly friendly; particularly in the smaller cities. As you visit each new city you will find that the locals take to you with a warm smile and an open heart, and will often be eager to help you when you look lost.

Mexico does of course have its own share of dangers, but this should not worry you or limit you in your exploration of this beautiful country. Each city is perfectly safe, as long as you can stick to the right areas and mix common sense into your sense of adventure!

I will outline exactly how to get the most out of each of the best cities throughout Mexico, and how to do this in a safe way. The adventures and exciting situations you will find yourself in throughout Mexico are countless, and I will allow you to experience them all.

What I hope to achieve in this book is to provide you with a reliable guide on exactly what to see in each of Mexico's major cities, and how to navigate your way around the country to see as much as humanly possible.

I will give you the top ten of my personal favorite things to see and do in each of the top ten cities in Mexico, as well as a description of exactly why you simply can't miss them. I will provide insights that I've gained from my own extensive travel throughout Mexico, and some tips for making the most out of your own Mexican adventure.

So allow me to show you the real Mexico - its sights, people and hidden treasures - and you will have the trip of a lifetime!

Chapter 1: Mazatlán

The only way to start any Mexican adventure is with a trip to the magical, romantic city of Mazatlán. A beach paradise, a humble ocean-side resort and a buzzing, eclectic Mexican town: Mazatlán is all this and more.

The local Mazatlecos will welcome you into their home with an air of happiness and warmth, and be glad to receive you into their haven. They'll tell you about the beaches, the food, the music and make you feel as if Mazatlán has been your home all of your life.

The city also has a rich history, one that you can feel as you walk its ancient streets and paths. There are museums and historic buildings to be seen, old cobblestone-lined alleys and squares to be visited and a culture which is rich and tangible.

The most amazing thing about this sleepy, sandy destination, though, is the experience of a red sun silhouette over its beaches, leading you into vibrant nights of partying beneath the star-lit night sky.

The Top Ten

Old Mazatlán - The Old Town of Mazatlán is a historical playground for locals and tourists. Walking its streets and courtyards provides the best first experience of the city, and allows you to get a true feel for the culture of the city and its people. The 19th century Cathedral is the highlight of the Old

Town, soaring high into the skyline with its tall, bright yellow towers and epic facade.

Teatro Ángelo Peralta - Another highlight located in the historic center of the city is the Peralta Theater, an amazing scene and an exciting night out for anyone who visits. After being restored at the end of the 20th century, the venue now boasts a wide range of concerts, movies and performances, and watching any of these from its high balconies is a magical experience.

Isla de la Piedra - For a quiet escape outside the realms of the main part of the city, there is no better place than Isla de la Piedra. Coconut trees abound and the white sand of the beach crunch beneath your toes as you walk the stretch of this magnificent beach. Watch the surfers carving up and down the face of waves on the shore, and kick back with a coconut in hand to enjoy the sunshine.

Explore the beaches - There are far too many amazing beaches surrounding Mazatlán to name them all, but there are a few more you shouldn't miss. Playa Olas Altas provides a pebbly beach that is not perfect for swimming, but provides an interesting look into a beach where tourism once was lively. Playa Norte is alive with joggers and beach goers constantly, while Playa Sábalo is generally more quiet and provides calm waters for swimming and frolicking. With more than 15 kms of beaches, you can spend days exploring the picturesque sands of Mazatlàn.

Museo de Arte - Art lovers and all appreciators of beauty will love the Museo de Arte. This humble museum provides a decent collection of Mexican art. With sculptures, paintings, prints and other works all providing a look through the history of Mexican innovation in the creative arts.

Molika - If all of your exploring is making you feel slightly peckish, the solution to your hunger woes can be found at Molika. With delicious salads, sandwiches and pastries, this hotspot is a favorite lunch and dinner hangout for both locals and tourists. It is a fantastic place to meet others who are resting from their own exploration of the city, too.

Punta de Clavadistas - A must-see show is provided by the brave, athletic cliff divers of Mazatlàn. Here locals risk life and limb to dive out over a spectacular rocky cliff face into the treacherous waters below, all for your own entertainment. They will ask for tips after their death-defying jump, but it is more than worth it for the show. If you're brave enough you may even be able to attempt the perilous leap yourself, but I wouldn't recommend it!

La Tertulia - As night falls there is only one form of beverage which you should be thinking about consuming: Tequila! La Tertulia provides the perfect venue for indulging in this Mexican delight, and the atmosphere is truly Mexican as well: with stuffed bull's heads lining the walls and bullfighting posters galore. This venue provides the perfect place to start a night out.

Fiesta Land - After a few tequila shots, you need something to do with your new found excitement and sudden urge to dance and Fiesta Land provides the perfect release. Fiesta Land is the undisputed center of partying in Mazatlán, with several hot night clubs and dance venues inside its white walls. The castle pumps out loud Latin music until the late hours of the night, and the open-air dance floor of Bora-Bora is a favorite on warmer nights.

El Quelite - The surrounding area of Mazatlán boasts some fantastic potential locations for day trips, but the number one destination is El Quelite. This small town is a picturesque area with thousands of amazing photo opportunities, delectable food venues and extremely tourist friendly. The top reasons to visit are for its array of rural food delicacies within its restaurants, and its lush, rich vegetation and abundance of beautiful flowered gardens.

Chapter 2: Puerto Vallarta

This city of sparkling blue water, vibrant beaches and hot tourist attractions has the potential to be a generic resort town and simple tourist luring destination, but it works hard to ensure it is so much more than that.

The city boasts an amazing assortment of local restaurants, shops and venues which remain unchanged by western influence. Walking through the city you will feel as if you have been allowed into something which is truly special: a Mexican city that is proud of its heritage and open for others to share in its customs.

The scenery is out of this world, too; with untouched stretches of beach, crystal blue waters and the backdrop of gray mountains cutting into the skyline behind the city. There is plenty to do in this haven to occupy your days here; from horse-back beach tours to all-day diving adventures, you will never have a dull moment in Puerto Vallarta.

The Top Ten

The Malecon - Walk the boardwalk of the Malecon, nearly a kilometer in length, along the shores of the sea and through the main sights and scenes of Puerto Vallarta. You will walk past the most popular bars, restaurants and shops, giving you a first-hand glimpse at some of the best spots to visit while staying in the city. It will give you the best first experience of the city and help you to become familiar and excited with the local delights the city has to offer.

Puerto Vallarta Market - Whether shopping for clothes, jewelry, rugs or accessories; the local municipal market has it all. There are a wide variety of hand-made souvenirs and trinkets on offer here, and on the second floor there is an array of fine food establishments allowing you to partake in local delicacies including tacos, chilies and shrimp broth.

The Main Plaza - A focal point of the city, the Main Plaza is an area constantly buzzing with people from every walk of life. There are regular presentations and art exhibits held here, but if nothing is on you can rest here and gaze about at the picturesque landscape of the mountainous backdrop or down toward the beautiful, blue ocean.

Rancho El Charro - Even if horseback riding on a picturesque beach is not your idea of fun, you simply must try it once at Rancho El Charro. Scenic tours which last several hours are reasonable well priced and provide an amazing experience as you witness more of the beautiful scenery of Puerto Vallarta than you ever could by foot. You will appreciate it so much that you may even develop a special bond with your pony companion.

Templo de Guadolupe - This magnificent structure that juts up into the sky from the heart of the city has become an icon for Puerto Vallarta. It's red facade provides amazing photo opportunities, especially in combination with surrounding cityscape.

Red Cabbage Café - Providing a vivid collection of recipes and local cuisines, this quaint little café is must to stop in for at least one meal. Their assortment of traditional local foods and indigenous sauces is a rarity, and one which must be experienced firsthand to appreciate the difference between this and other acclaimed traditional Mexican dishes. The taste combinations are so unique; you'll find yourself ordering several meals just so you can try everything.

Los Arcos - With a seaside backdrop combined with a series of grand arches that look like a work of art, this outdoor amphitheater is a popular spot for all locals and tourists in Puerto Vallarta. Becoming somewhat of a symbol for the city, the shows here are engaging and unique, and night time spectaculars provide an intimate look into the culture of the city.

Birdwatching - The entire surrounding area of Puerto Vallarta provides prime opportunity for glimpsing hundreds of species of birds. The dense jungle which surrounds the harbor provides the perfect setting to explore, with binoculars in hand, to seek out some rare and vibrant bird species.

Mismaloya - To the south of Puerto Vallarta lies Mismaloya; a beautifully serene beach surrounded by lush jungle. With an array of amazing spots to swim or splash about, as well as a selection of small restaurants to experience divine Mexican seafood dishes, you won't regret visiting this area.

Vallarta Botanical Gardens - Located a short distance south of the city, the Botanical Gardens provide an awe-inspiring experience filled with natural beauty. You will be consumed by the wild palms, orchids, ferns and lush vegetation which the gardens consist of. If walking through the dense vegetation is warming you up, take a dip in the refreshing, pristine waters of the river which runs through the gardens.

Chapter 3: Guanajuato

The picturesque city of Guanajuato has many ups and downs, physically speaking. Residing on hilly terrain high in the mountains, almost every street of this amazing city is on a slant, making for a fun experience to travel around.

The scenery within this mountainous area is simply breathtaking, and Guanajuato is constantly regarded as the most beautiful city in Mexico. While in stark contrast to the many beach littered cities on Mexico's coast, Guanajuato provides a different, equally enjoyable experience for tourists.

Originating as a silver and gold-mining centrality, many of the silver mines surrounding the city are still in use today. The wealth from such activities has flown into the city, and many of the buildings and structures are a vibrant, colorful assortment of architectural wonder. Walking through this UNESCO World Heritage Site is a true delight, and you won't be able to get enough of its vibrant culture.

The Top Ten

Calejón del Beso - As you begin exploring the many winding, narrow and slanted streets and alleys the Gunanajuato possesses, be sure to stumble upon Calejón del Beso. This is the narrowest of the alleys in the city, and as you squeeze between the houses along it you'll get the chance to view some locals going about their daily lives: hanging washing from their near-touching balconies and conversing in vibrant, lively Spanish.

Museo Regional de Guanajuato Alhóndiga de Granaditas - Being the site of the first major victory of the rebels in Mexico's War of Independence, this mouthful of a museum combines art and history to paint a picture of the tale of Mexico as a whole, as well as the local area and its influence upon the country. The Alhóndiga was first a grain storehouse, then a fortress, later an armory, before becoming a school, a prison and finally the museum it is today!

Museo de las Momias - A museum of a different type is the Museo de las Momias. This museum provides an intriguing insight of Mexico's fascination with and even celebration of death. It enables visitors to view more than 100 corpses, all possessing the look of mummified remains, inclusive of warped bodies and horrid expressions upon their faces. The museum is fascinating if nothing else and highly recommended to visit.

Café Tal - Mexico isn't exactly renowned for its coffees or abundance of experienced baristas, but Café Tal pays no attention to this fact. This grungy location is always overflowing with coffee enthusiasts, particularly tourists who are craving a good drop of coffee.

Universidad de Guanajuato - Providing one of the most outstanding architectural wonders in the city is the local university. Its ramparts can be seen from far away, high above much of the city. Its white and blue facade is in contrast to much of the architecture in the rest of the city, and some despise it for looking out of place. You have to appreciate its boldness, though, making a point towards progression of the city into the modern era.

Templo la Valenciana - One of the more spectacular sights of Guanajuato is the Templo la Valencia. Sitting high upon a hill overlooking the city, it provides an amazing view out across the city. The interior is decorated with golden altars and paintings, and its exterior is a dazzling display spectacularly ornate.

The Silver Mines - You would be amiss if you did not experience the history of Guanajuato firsthand, by visiting s few of the Silver Mines surrounding the city. San Ramón allows you to descend deep into its caverns, to a depth of 60m into the dark if you are brave enough. San Cayetano is another mine which is great for tourists, with a museum and guided tours by former miners who explain the history and importance of the mines to the city.

Las Mercedes - In a quaint area overlooking the sleepy Guanajuato rests one of the city's finest dining establishments. It provides quintessential local dishes that take hours to prepare, ready just in time for the evening dinner rush. Providing a romantic dining experience, the venue is constantly packed with loving couples, and reservations are recommended.

Teatro Juárez - This magnificent theater is over a century old and has provided first-rate entertainment since its construction in the late nineteenth century. Inside the structure is a grand display of interior design and lavish decor, and outside is just as grandiose. Leaving the city without visiting this ostentatious venue would be a true shame.

El Capitolio - The sleepy city of Guanajuato comes alive at the hottest club in the city: El Capitolio. Pumping out techno and house music at all hours of the night, Capitolio is a popular destination for all party-goers, while still remaining an elegant and refined air about it. This is surprising considering their constantly cheap drink deals and popularity with the younger crowd.

Chapter 4: San Miguel de Allende

The magic which the city of San Miguel de Allende exudes will captivate you immediately, putting you under its spell and leaving you wondering why you would ever want to leave. With a vibrant culture, eclectic shops and venues and a magic feel in each crack and crevice of this wonderful city, it may just be your favorite Mexican city.

The weather is always perfect in San Miguel de Allende, which has been described as possessing an eternal spring. It is beautiful and unique in every aspect, with a culture to be found nowhere else and the people being some of the friendliest in the entire world.

The streets are designed in such a way that they are an utter pleasure to walk upon, they are lined with wonderful sights and there is an abundance of fantastic local shops and restaurants to enjoy.

Perhaps the most enjoyable experience the city has to offer is in the subtlety of the setting sun over the many open rooftops the buildings of San Miguel de Allende possess. As you sit upon them and watch the colors of the day blend with the palette of the night sky, your worries too will fade with the setting sun.

The Top Ten

El Mirador - For a breathtaking glimpse over the city, to put this beautiful city into perspective before you begin exploring it in detail, El Mirador provides the best view. After looking out across the city and its countless rooftops, take a path down to Parque Benito Juárez, a shaded park which is a fantastic spot to stop for a rest and to relax.

El Charco del Ingenio - A park of a slightly grander scale, these botanical gardens provide an excellent place to visit to lose yourself in nature. There is an abundance of native plants to be seen, as well as animals within this wildlife sanctuary. You could easily spend an entire day here and not run out of things to see and vibrant plants to experience.

Parroquia de San Miguel Arcángel - This grand structure is one of the most vibrant and unforgettable structures to be experienced in the city. Rocketing into the sky with its pointy, pink spires, this parish church is remarkable in its design and can be seen from miles away. The bright pink facade is the highlight of the building, but the interior is impressive also.

Museo del Juguete Popular Mexicano - While designed specifically for children, don't let this small fact stop you from visiting this exciting museum. Showcasing every type of toy that has ever existed throughout the history of Mexican culture, this museum feels like a a cartoon adventure that you've somehow stumbled into. The toys will make you wish that you were a kid again, if only so that you didn't feel so guilty about not sharing them with the other children visiting.

Café Rama - A wonderful combination of a café mixed with a bar mixed with a restaurant, this venue has a little something for everyone. Visit for a coffee in the afternoon, a relaxing drink at night or a delicious meal in the early evening. The local types that visit here will inspire you to find out more about the city, and other tourists will share stories with you of their adventures so far.

Escuela de Bellas Artes - Originating as a monastery in former times, the building was transformed into a school of fine arts, one which still offers several courses to this day. For those not looking to improve their artistic talents, but view the fruits of the talent of others, the murals within the building are fantastic and engaging. There are regular, temporary exhibits of different forms throughout the year as well.

San Agustín - For those with a particularly sweet tooth, or several of them, San Agustín should not be missed. Offering some of the most delicious treats to be found anywhere, their churros and chocolates are both rich and utterly satisfying; just don't eat too many before dinner!

Biblioteca Pública - Whether you are a bookworm or not, you would be making a mistake not to visit this large, expansive library. With a collection of books that is one of the largest English collections in Latin America, the library is an epicenter for learning. It is also somewhat of a cultural center, acting as a meeting point for various groups and assortments of people.

El Manantial - For dinner with a show, El Manantial is the place to go. Although the show isn't provided unless you can convince a friend to try their ultra spicy chili sauce! If you can find an amigo brave enough to cover their meal in their famous sauce, sit back and wait for hilarity to ensue. This former saloon is also a great place for a few cocktails and light conversation.

Mama Mía - A venue with a slightly more electric buzz to it, Mama Mía boasts karaoke most nights of the week. As locals take turns at sacrificing their pride, they take the stage to sing a local favorite or an American classic, to be in turn ridiculed by theirs fellow amigos. It is fantastic value and only gets better as the night goes on.

Chapter 5: Mexico City

The largest metropolis within the confines of the Mexican borders, and the most busy, buzzing and action-filled city as a result, is undoubtedly Mexico City. Constantly berated as a center of crime and a 'dirty city', it is beginning to clean up its act in a big way.

The war on drugs in Mexico is far from over, but Mexico City is now far safer than it has been in decades, and you shouldn't let the rumors of danger keep you away from this fantastic city. You simply can't fully appreciate the history and culture of Mexico without visiting this exciting capital.

The culinary scene is alive and well in Mexico City, with some of the most esteemed restaurants in the entire country. The cantinas, shops, street stalls and roads are rife with chaos at any moment of the day, but this experience is an exciting one to experience, so long as you are vigilant and have your wits about you. While admittedly the busy nature of the city is not for everyone, this is Mexico at its core and is a must-see city for anyone wanting the entire Mexican experience.

The Top Ten

Plaza de las Tres Culturas - This popular square is rich with culture and history, representing the amalgamation of pre-Hispanic and Spanish influences in this Mexican capital. The plaza displays a typically Aztec influence, and is an architectural wonder as well as an intriguing cultural experience.

Palacio de Bellas Artes - A work of art, both inside and out, the Palacio de Bellas Artes is an inspiring structure. With an austere, white marble facade that dominates the skyline, you will be drawn towards it from afar. Inside you will find enormous, colorful murals that will hold your glance for minutes at a time, in combination with various other artistic exhibits including several on contemporary architecture.

Salón Tenampa - Another venue possessing rich, engaging murals, but of a slightly more humble existence, is Salón Tenampa. This local cantina provides an exciting and fun-filled experience as you bop your head along to the whimsical tunes in this humble Mexican venue.

Palacio Nacional - One of the most iconic attractions to be found in Mexico City, this colonial palace is the birthplace of many of the policies and laws that have made Mexico what it is today. It is the home to the office of the President of Mexico, and so under high guard at all times, but it is a popular tourist destination to visit. The halls of the building include several fascinating murals, and the exterior of the building is as impressive as any other in Mexico City.

Arena México - If you have ever seen the fanciful masks adorned by Mexican wrestlers in movies, and thought that it was fictional creation, think again. This 17,000 seat arena hosts epic face-offs between the heavyweights of Mexican wrestling weekly. With blood, sweat and tears the wrestlers fight to the loud cheers of the local crowd: an exciting experience to say the least!

Mercado de la Merced - You may be confused that you've stumbled into a city separate from the one you were just within, into one consisting of streets of fresh produce, buildings in the form of street stalls and all the denizens happening to be street vendors! La Merced Market is like a city of its own, constantly abuzz with haggling for the freshest produce and ingredients to be put in the evening chili.

Monumento a la Revolución - The plaza within which this grand monument to the revolution of Mexico resides is a fantastic spot to visit, alive with people of all walks of life. The monument itself is impressive, with the highlight being the 65m-high observation deck that juts out for a pristine view of the surrounding city.

Pujol - What is widely regarded as Mexico's finest dining establishment, this famed restaurant is booked out well in advance. If you are a fan of exquisite in any capacity, you simply can't miss this dining experience. Mixing traditional Mexican cuisine with a contemporary twist, the meals are a true delight and well worth reserving a table in advance if you are organized enough - its an experience you won't regret.

Plaza Garibaldi - If you are a fan of traditional Mexican mariachi bands, you will love Plaza Garibaldi. In true flamboyant Mexican style they play hearty tunes with trumpets and guitars, approaching the odd spectator to serenade. With their dazzling outfits gleaming in the moonlight while their music echoing across the square, the performances are not to be missed.

Centro Cultural de España - A capital city is nothing without some proper nighttime entertainment, and this can be found at Centro Cultural de España. This pumping nightclub is a favorite for its consistently entertaining selection of live acts and DJs, providing one of the best music scenes to be found in Mexico City.

Chapter 6: Oaxaca

The culture and traditions of this warm, friendly city run deeper than most of the other major Mexican cities. Filled with amazing indigenous traditions still to this day, Oaxaca provides a cultural experience that is not to be found anywhere else.

It feels as if there is a light constantly shining upon this great city, and there is a creative air felt all throughout it. This feeling runs deep within its inhabitants, inspiring them to create remarkable artworks and unique culinary dishes. The streets of Oaxaca always boast some form of colorful activity; whether it is a street vendor selling colorful trinkets or foods, or a traditional dance routine performed for onlookers.

The city itself is immersed in indigenous culture, being surrounded by archaeological sites and ruins, and there are plenty of opportunities to visit these via various modes of transport, ranging from hiking to horseback riding.

The real delight of this hidden gem, however, is its people. The vast majority possess very little in terms of personal wealth, but they are never lacking a broad smile and a warm, welcoming heart.

The Top Ten

Templo de Santo Domingo - Of the many spectacular churches littered throughout Oaxaca - and there are many - the Templo de Santo Domingo has to be the most beautiful to behold. With the facade boasting a lavish Baroque look, it is inviting to all that look upon it. Inside the church the true magic is found, however. Painted figures are found throughout the interior and there is a glow of gold everywhere you look. The warm glow is accentuated in the candlelit ceremonies held in the evening.

Museo de las Culturas de Oaxaca - The Museum of Oaxacan Cultures, sitting right beside the Templo de Santo Domingo and within a gorgeous monastery, provides a rich look into the culture of the city and its history. It provides a look back into the time line of the city, from pre-Hispanic up until the present day.

Museo Rufino Tamayo - This museum provides a distinctly different experience, instead focusing on ancient artworks and artifacts of the city and surrounding area. The pieces are extremely unique and unlike any other pieces even to be found within other Mexican cities, and there are some real treasures within the walls of the museum.

Benito Juárez Market - Oaxaca City boasts some fantastically vibrant markets, with one of the finest being the Benito Juárez Market. With hundreds of stalls mixing together smells, sights and sounds from each of the individual foods and wares for sale, the experience of walking through this market will make you feel truly alive. A highly recommended experience to partake in is to taste the local delicacy sold by many stalls: crunchy grasshoppers!

Zócalo - The streets of Oaxaco are lined with lush, green leaves and shaded by the many branches of the trees that hold them. The Zócalo is one of the best examples of this, providing a shaded center of activity that bustles with excitement all day long. There are bands, buskers, tourists and locals floating through the area, and an array of sidewalk cafes to sit and watch the people and the day pass by.

La Olla - A magnificent spot for breakfast or lunch, this local delight provides Oaxacan specialties that will delight the taste buds. The fish quesadillas are a real treat, along with the beef in mole chicilo. The venue itself provides the perfect hangout for meeting other tourists, as well as the odd local who can speak a little English.

Monte Albán - One of the more impressive sights to be witnessed in Oaxaca, and indeed in Mexico, is Monte Albán. These ancient ruins lie just a few kilometers west of the city, sitting above a flattened hilltop. This former Zapotec capital provides stunning panoramic views and possesses a vast number of largely intact ruins to explore.

Palacio de Gobierno - Murals are a recurring theme among many of the more notable Mexican buildings, especially so in the Palacio de Gobierno. This State government Palace, constructed of spectacular marble, also holds the world's largest tortilla. The large art piece, 300kg in weight, is decorated with the history of Mexico.

La Biznaga - This local courtyard possesses an amazingly inviting atmosphere, with locals and tourists alike crammed into its vicinity for some of the finest food in Oaxaca. The dishes are all strictly of Oaxacan influence, delighting all those who taste them. There is also a range of draft micro brew beer on offer to wash the delicious food down.

Txalaparta - This bar is the perfect place to go to let loose or to chill out from the early afternoon all the way into the evening. At midnight the bar transforms into a dancing haven, with locals dancing to hip-hop, reggae and Latin music all throughout the night. The party atmosphere is contagious, and you may find yourself coming back here several times throughout your stay in this wonderful city.

Chapter 7: Merida

A city ingrained deep within the history of Mexico since the Spanish conquest, Mérida is now a capital of culture across the entire Mexican peninsula. This is the ultimate location to begin your journey throughout the Yucatán state, but one in which you won't be willing to leave in a hurry.

The central area of the city possesses a high concentration of fantastic eating venues, bars, shops and markets, and the city has one of the highest densities of quality museums in Mexico. Wandering through the streets it is easy to get lost, which is not a bad thing, as you explore its many plazas and narrow lanes that will lead you to your next amazing discovery.

It is a large metropolis, unlike many of the surrounding beach-side resort towns, but it is one with a small-town feel. It is possible to go down the classic tourist route, seeing all the flashy highlights the city has to offer, or to embed yourself more thoroughly in the city to get the local feel; the choice is up to you.

The Top Ten

Catedral de San Ildefonso - This gigantic, domineering cathedral is hard to miss when you enter Mérida, blocking the sky as you gaze up toward it. The interior is less remarkable than the exterior, being of a more minimalistic design than other ostentatious churches. It does, however, host Mérida's most esteemed religious artifact: the statue Cristo de las Ampollas, said to have been burnt in a natural fire for an entire night without burning.

Casa de Montejo - A former mansion for the wealthy families that resided within the dwelling, Casa de Montejo now exists as a museum displaying the lavish furnishings of the building. It is the exterior that is the true marvel, however. The facade displays conquistadors and priests immortalized in the statues that represent them.

Iglesia de Jésus - This quaint stone church pales in comparison by size to the mighty cathedral, but is equally remarkable to visit. The stones used to build the church were gathered from the remnants of a destroyed Maya temple around 400 years ago.

Gran Museo del Mundo Maya - This particular museum embodies the rich Mayan culture more than any other in the state. Possessing over 500 individual Maya artifacts on display, visitors are able to get a sense of how art played a part in their culture and community, and how the race progressed as a people through the informative guided tour.

La Chaya Maya - A classic Yucatán cuisine experience awaits you at La Chaya Maya. Their specialty dish of choice (and the choice of most visitors) is the delectable slow-cooked pork. This restaurant is favorite for locals even more so than tourists, which really says something about how it upholds the traditional flavors of the region.

Museo de Arte Popular de Yucatán - Another fantastic museum that is well worth visiting is the Museo de Arte Popular de Yucatán. This stunning building has intriguing displays of popular art from every corner of Mexico, and has regularly changing feature exhibits. The collection of artwork, textiles and

Mexican handcrafts are extremely versatile and the history of their evolution in Mexican culture is fascinating.

Parque Santa Lucía - This quiet yet stunning little park is a winner for all those looking for a peaceful reprieve. Sitting on the grass here and watching the locals pass by is a real treat, as you watch them weave in and out of little shops and between the other denizens. On sunny days this park is particularly cheerful, but it is fun to visit on any occasion.

Plaza Grande - Another local hotspot to visit is the Plaza Grande. This center square is often overflowing with people throughout the day, all coming and going from different locations. Each day there is a ceremony held here in which the Mexican flag is hoisted into the air, and nearly every evening there is live music to enjoy. Throughout the day you can enjoy Plaza Grande by relaxing on a shady bench and watching the clouds roll by.

Mayan Pub - Every city has to have a raucous club overflowing with backpackers and young locals, and the Mayan Pub fits the bill in Mérida. This pub comes stocked with a beer garden, live music and a promise of good times to be had. It's the best place in town to meet other young travelers as well as locals out to have a good time.

Uxmal - A spectacular historical location within a few hours' drive of Mérida delivers one of the most amazing experiences to be had in the Yucatán state. Uxmal is an ancient Mayan city that possesses some of the grandest and stunning structures the Mayans ever created. The grand pyramid which stands at the middle is one of the largest in Mexico, and the surrounding ruins are remarkable also.

Chapter 8: Cancún

White sand beaches, scorching sun and refreshing, cool ocean water to frolic in all day long. This is just the beginning of what Cancún has to offer. The beaches in Cancún make it a popular destination for tourists to travel to all year around, and the party scene is an added draw card.

But once you enter this electric city, you will discover that Cancún is so much more than a typical resort town. Roaming the streets is a never-ending adventure, as you stumble upon bars, clubs and venues with ceaselessly inspiring Latin sounds that will have you moving like you never have before.

An eternal summer is cast over Cancún, with everyday being another opportunity to laze on the beach, enjoy the poolside and laugh in the sunshine. The surrounding area of Cancún has its fair share of delights as well, and a simple day trip can get you in touch with an unforgettable natural experience.

Your days in Cancun will be spent with a cocktail in one hand, grains of sand running through the other, and a broad smile permanently stuck upon your face.

The Top Ten

Playa Langosta - For an immediate taste of Cancún's famed white sand beaches, look no further than Playa Langosta. This beach is pure heaven, with snow white sand and clear, shallow water that is perfect for the odd spot of swimming or snorkeling. The only danger here is that you spend too long relaxing in the sun!

Museo Maya de Cancún - This transfixing museum houses some of the rarest Mayan artifacts to ever have been found, and provides an utterly engaging experience. Ceramics and sculptures make up the majority of the hundreds of pieces of the rare collection, with some ancient jewelery also included in the exhibits. The museum provides an interesting look back into the lives of the ancient Mayan race which once inhabited the land.

Yamil Lu'um - The Scorpion's Temple, as it is also known, is not so much a temple anymore as a set of ruins. It is, however, remarkable to look upon and well worth the trip to find it from the beach. It overlooks the ocean and creates a pleasurable viewing experience as you gaze upon the ruins and imagine what it must have been like in its former glory.

San Miguelito - Another of the many famous archaeological Mayan sites to be found in Cancún and its surrounding area, San Miguelito several Mayan structures that have been standing for hundreds of years, now restored to their previous beauty. A tour of these buildings gives you a more grounded feeling of what it could have been like living in the ancient Mayan culture.

Playa Tortugas - Spring break is found all year long at the wild, loud and exciting Playa Tortugas. This pumping beach is constantly packed with people of all ages running about, playing sports, listening to music and enjoying each other's company. There are a plenitude of fantastic restaurants in the area to stop into for a bite to eat if the partying happens to work up an appetite.

Isla Mujeres - A half-hour boat ride from Cancún rests a fantastic island experience: one where golf carts are the main mode of transportation. The island provides a more relaxed vibe than Cancún, and provides the amazing highlight of a legitimate turtle farm. This sanctuary releases tens of thousands of baby turtles every year, which must fight their way to the water in order to survive.

MUSA - Ever wondered what an art museum would look like underwater? You don't have to wonder any more, as MUSA provides this exact experience. Dive beneath the surface of the water to experience this underwater sculpture museum, with around 400 stunning pieces to view. These concrete figures are eerily realistic, and as you swim past you may half expect them to reach out and grab you!

Checándole - For the most exquisite food in all of Cancún, there is no competition with Checándole. Their food is delectable and the atmosphere is always conducive to an enjoyable time. One of their most delightful specialties is a dish of chicken dripping with melted chocolate and chili sauce, and it's every bit as delightful as it sounds.

Chichen Itza - A few hours from the city of Cancún resides the piece de resistance of the ancient Mayan race: Chichen Itza. The ancient capital of the mighty Mayan Empire houses one of the Seven Wonders of the World, the mighty pyramid of Chichen Itza. This structure is captivating and powerful, as is the entire ancient city and every structure within it. A tour of this area is a must for any tourist even remotely curious of this fascinating culture.

Cenote Ik Kil - This hidden cave sinkhole is like something out of a Hollywood movie: a deep circular cavern in the middle of the jungle filled with crystal blue water. You can only begin to imagine how perfect it is until you arrive here yourself. This cenote is open to the public for swimming, and is constantly filled with eager tourists and locals. The most spectacular part of this experience is looking up at the open sky above you as you're surrounded by vines and cave walls.

Chapter 9: Cozumel

While many may regard Cozumel purely as yet another stop on the resort trail for tourists, they are sorely mistaken. This proud little city has a lot to offer, and makes a point to show it to anyone who happens to land on its shores.

There is a vast array of opportunities to explore the amazing ocean surrounding Cozumel; both its reefs and the beautiful animals they contain. The snorkeling and diving scene here is one of the cheapest and most rewarding in the world, showing a spectrum of colors unlike anything you will have seen before.

The beaches are less crowded than in the surrounding, larger party cities, enabling a serene experience in which you can kick back, relax and think of what's really important in your life. Taking a short trip out of the city will remove you even further from civilization, and allow you to experience hidden beaches and treasures of the Mexican coast. Relax and embrace all that is Cozumel.

The Top Ten

Palancar Reef - The coral reefs surrounding Cozumel provide a look into marine micro habitats at an up close and personal level. Palancar Reef is one of the best to experience these microcosms, with vibrantly colorful coral and a dazzling array of fish always present.

Santa Rosa Wall - If you've had a little more experience with diving, the Santa Rosa Wall provides a deeper look into the fantastic marine life surrounding

Cozumel. This wall dive can be a little intimidating if you are not experienced, but is well worth it, particularly for the cave at the end of the dive!

Columbia Reef - Sea turtles, sharks and fish of all sizes is what you can expect to find at Columbia Reef! This diving experience offers a vast display of fantastic creatures that are not shy to get in your face and even graze your skin as they swim past. The water is so clear that you can see unobstructed for well ahead of you, gazing through coral and down to the ocean floor at crawling lobsters and crabs, and fish lurking beneath you.

Havana Bob's Cuban Cigars - Upon your return to dry land, you ought to reward yourself for your brave dive into the depths of the ocean. The best way to do this is by experiencing one of Havana Bob's premium Cuban cigars! Relax as you puff on one of Bob's fine, rolled cigars as he teaches you a little bit about the history of cigars, or tells a riveting story about his own experience with them!

El Castillo Real - Although not as grand in appearance as the mighty Chichen Itza, El Castillo Real provides another Mayan ruins experience to enjoy. This former royal castle now lies in ruins, but retains much of its structure. The structure is nothing compared to its former glory, but a fun adventure can be had in traveling to see these ruins.

San Gervasio - These nearby ruins are slightly better preserved than El Castillo Real, but also pale in comparison to other ruins on the mainland. Still, they provide an interesting experience to wander through, particularly when the story behind the ruins is told, of it being the site of the sanctuary of the God of Fertility.

Playa Palancar - One of the few beaches on Cozumel which is not over-commercialized, this relaxing beach provides the ideal place to relax and enjoy a few cervezas. Restaurants and bars surround the area, so you'll never go hungry or thirsty while kicking back on the beach.

El Mirador - This is the typical picture-perfect viewpoint of the island: a section of cliff protruding outward from the land with waves crashing violently against the rock. if you get your timing right, the photo opportunities are endless. Just be careful walking out across the sharp rock-face; shoes are recommended!

Mr Sanchos Beach Club - For a full day of catering, fun and relaxation, Mr Sanchos is the perfect option. Even if you are not usually into being pampered or having everything taken care of for you, this beach club will offer you an experience you will be hard-pressed to reject. With excellent food, massages and amazing cocktails, you should allow yourself one day to be pampered at this fantastic day resort.

The Money Bar - A fun atmosphere and deliciously refreshing drinks is what you can find at The Money Bar. The vibe here is super relaxed, as you chill out by the ocean, with a breathtaking view and amongst great company. It's an amazing way to spend any afternoon or evening, and you may find yourself returning here several times before leaving Cozumel.

Chapter 10: Tulum

Back to the mainland and back to yet another magical Mexican beach city. Tulum shares a lot in common with the other cities along the coastline of southern Mexico: perfect water, pristine beaches and a relaxed vibe. What makes it unique is the more humble city center which welcomes people from all walks of life to enjoy its cheap restaurants and accommodation.

Outside of the city center sit the odd hidden beach shack, a set of Mayan ruins and colorful coral. If you so desire you can travel either way along the coast to experience yet more fantastic beaches and even some more hidden swimming holes that will take your breath away.

Tulum is a tropical paradise just waiting to invite you in for a warm tropical kiss. Countless adventures await you upon your arrival as you spend your time exploring white sandy beaches and laying back beneath starry skies in the warm evenings. Time will seem to stand still in Tulum; only it won't. So make the most of this amazing city while you can!

The Top Ten

Tulum Ruins - The Mayan ruins of Tulum are unique not because of the structure of the ruins themselves, but because of their location. They have the most magnificent surroundings imaginable: upon the cliff overlooking clear, turquoise waters and a stretch of white sandy beach. Gazing out across the water from the ruins you can imagine that the previous inhabitants must have felt quite content with their living conditions.

Playa Paraiso - Surrounded by beautiful palm trees, sitting upon warm, white sand and daydreaming at the bright blue water in front of you: is this paradise? This is the thought that will come to mind while sitting on Playa Paraiso. Watching the fishing boats go about their daily business is an added bonus to relaxing on this fantastic beach.

Tulum Bazaar - Take a stroll through the local bazaar and peruse the fine wares on offer from the friendliest and most hospitable vendors in town. All prices can be bargained down, as they usually begin quite high to catch tourists out. Be sure to check whether the items are made locally as well, as these are the true treasures and there can be many fake items that are not worth much value.

Tulum Monkey Sanctuary - The monkeys within this sanctuary certainly aren't shy, and you'll be able to spot a multitude of them upon first arrival. The monkeys are constantly running about, playing with visitors and mischievously stealing food from their open hands. Feeding the monkeys is a sheer delight, and as they swing on the trees above you, you can really get a sense of being deep in the Mayan jungle.

El Mariachi Loco - A simple, yet tantalizing taste experience is provided by El Mariachi Loco. This popular restaurant provides succulent cuts of meat to its visitors, a range of simple, delicious dishes and a welcoming atmosphere. The grilled fish which is sourced locally is a real treat, and at a great price too.

Batey Mojito & Guarapo Bar - An authentic, traditional Mexican bar with delicious drinks and an ambient atmosphere. That is what you can expect to find at the Batey Mojito & Guarapo Bar. The mezcal is the best of the region, but the mojitos are the real treat. Each one is freshly made from the sugary syrup of the sugar cane at the bar, and the result is a smooth and sweet taste sensation that will knock your socks off!

Sistema Dos Ojos - An amazing underwater adventure awaits you at the Sistema Dos Ojos. This underwater cave formation provides an unforgettable snorkeling experience, made even more amazing if you also have the qualifications to dive even deeper. There is also an eerie bat cave to explore if you have your wits about you!

Temple of Doom - Jumping into a dark hole into the Temple of Doom beneath is not something which sounds very alluring. But it is! Once you jump through this daunting opening you find yourself submerged in fresh, clear, blue water hidden but for a small opening to the sunlight above. After jumping in you can float around and enjoy yourself in the small aqueous space; just make sure you clear the path for jumpers after you.

Punta Laguna Natural Reserve - This nature park has more actities to keep you busy than a theme park! There's canoing, zip lining, wildlife watching and swimming all available within a few meters of each other, and the activities are suitable for all ages. A day can easily be spent exploring this reserve without running out of things to do or parts to explore.

Coba Ruins - A decent hike through rough terrain lands you at the foot of these remarkable ruins. They provide a more interesting and less crowded experience than the Tulum Ruins, and there is a lot more to explore. The huge pyramid is the star attraction, and climbing to the top to take in the view of the surrounding ruins is undoubtedly the most rewarding experience the Tulum area has to offer.

Conclusion

Mexico is a truly unique country full of amazing people to meet and experiences to be had. Unfortunately for most people, seeing the whole of Mexico's wonderfully diverse country from top to bottom isn't a realistic option.

What I hope to have achieved with this book is to have provided you with a guide how to get the most out of Mexico in whatever time you have to spend exploring it. I would encourage you to stay here for as long as possible and soak up everything the country has to offer; the cities, the people, the culture and every unforgettable experience. But if you can't, just make sure that you don't miss any of the cities I've mentioned and try to get to each of the sights I've listed.

If you can make this round trip of Mexico and get to all of the sights mentioned, I can guarantee you that you will have had the experience of a lifetime, and will have captured a significant glimpse of Mexico's undeniably picturesque cities, landscape, architecture, powerful history and evocative culture.

I have no doubt that you will return at some stage in the future, hungry to see more of the beautiful, diverse and unforgettable country that is Mexico.

Finally, if you enjoyed this book, please take the time to share your thoughts and post a review on Amazon. I would really appreciate it if you did.

Thank you and happy travels!

The information herein is offered for informational purposes solely, and is universal as so. The presentation of the information is without contract or any type of guarantee assurance.

The trademarks that are used are without any consent, and the publication of the trademark is without permission or backing by the trademark owner. All trademarks and brands within this book are for clarifying purposes only and are the owned by the owners themselves, not affiliated with this document.

Made in the USA
San Bernardino, CA
06 January 2016